PRINCEWILL LAGANG

Mindful Partnership: Practicing Presence in Relationships

First published by PRINCEWILL LAGANG 2023

Copyright © 2023 by Princewill Lagang

All rights reserved. No part of this publication may be reproduced, stored or transmitted in any form or by any means, electronic, mechanical, photocopying, recording, scanning, or otherwise without written permission from the publisher. It is illegal to copy this book, post it to a website, or distribute it by any other means without permission.

Princewill Lagang asserts the moral right to be identified as the author of this work.

First edition

This book was professionally typeset on Reedsy.
Find out more at reedsy.com

Contents

1	Introduction	1
2	The Foundations of Mindfulness	4
3	Cultivating Self-Awareness	7
4	Active Listening and Communication	10
5	Emotional Intelligence and Empathy	13
6	Navigating Conflict Mindfully	16
7	Mindful Intimacy	19
8	Letting Go of Expectations	22
9	Balancing Individuality and Togetherness	25
10	Mindful Decision-Making	28
11	Creating Mindful Rituals	32
12	Sustaining a Mindful Partnership	36

1

Introduction

In a world bustling with rapid communication and constant connectivity, the art of cultivating meaningful and fulfilling partnerships often takes a backseat. The frantic pace of modern life has left many individuals yearning for genuine connections that transcend the superficial and provide a sense of deep-rooted understanding. This is where the concept of mindful partnership emerges, offering a refreshing perspective on how we can enrich our relationships and foster profound connections.

The Essence of Mindful Partnership

Mindful partnership refers to the intentional practice of being fully present and engaged in a relationship, with an open heart and non-judgmental awareness. It involves the conscious choice to invest time and effort into understanding one another on a deeper level, valuing the uniqueness of each individual, and nurturing the growth of the relationship as a whole. This approach encourages partners to embrace vulnerability, empathy, and compassion, creating a solid foundation for enduring bonds.

The Significance of Mindful Partnership

MINDFUL PARTNERSHIP: PRACTICING PRESENCE IN RELATIONSHIPS

In a world marked by the frenetic pace of daily life, mindful partnership offers a counterbalance that redefines the way we perceive and engage with our significant others. By actively incorporating mindfulness into our relationships, we pave the way for authenticity and emotional intimacy. This significance is underscored by the following key points:

1. Enhanced Communication: Mindful partnership encourages open and effective communication. Partners who practice mindfulness are more attuned to their own thoughts and emotions, allowing them to communicate their needs and desires more clearly. Moreover, they are better equipped to actively listen to their partners, fostering an environment of mutual respect and understanding.

2. Conflict Resolution: Mindfulness equips individuals with the tools to manage conflict in a constructive manner. When both partners are mindful, they approach conflicts with patience and empathy, seeking resolution rather than assigning blame. This approach transforms disagreements into opportunities for growth and learning.

3. Intimacy and Connection: Mindful partnership lays the groundwork for deeper intimacy and connection. The practice of being present with one another fosters a sense of emotional closeness that goes beyond physical proximity. This emotional bond is essential for creating a lasting and fulfilling partnership.

4. Personal Growth: Individual growth is an integral part of any partnership. Mindful partners support each other's personal development by providing a safe space for exploration and growth. This mutual encouragement fosters an environment where both partners can thrive as individuals and as a unit.

5. Stress Reduction: The practice of mindfulness in partnership can alleviate stress and anxiety. By focusing on the present moment, partners can find solace and support in one another, even during challenging times. This shared

INTRODUCTION

mindfulness helps to create a buffer against the stresses of life.

In the pages that follow, we will delve deeper into the nuances of mindful partnership, exploring practical strategies and exercises that can be employed to infuse mindfulness into your relationships. By embracing this approach, you embark on a journey towards more meaningful connections, emotional richness, and a harmonious balance between the demands of modern life and the profound bonds we all seek.

2

The Foundations of Mindfulness

In a world often consumed by the past or future, the practice of mindfulness emerges as a powerful tool to anchor us in the present moment. Mindfulness, at its core, is the art of cultivating conscious awareness and an accepting presence, allowing us to engage with life more fully and authentically. This chapter delves into the essence of mindfulness, its practical applications, and the fundamental principles that underpin its practice.

Defining Mindfulness

Mindfulness can be understood as the intentional act of paying attention to the present moment without judgment. It involves bringing a non-reactive and curious awareness to our thoughts, emotions, sensations, and surroundings. By doing so, we step away from the autopilot mode that often dominates our lives, enabling us to savor the richness of each moment and respond thoughtfully rather than impulsively.

Mindfulness in Everyday Life

While mindfulness has ancient roots in contemplative traditions, its application in modern life is invaluable. By incorporating mindfulness into our daily routines, we enhance our capacity to experience life in its entirety. From the simplest tasks like sipping a cup of tea to engaging in complex conversations, mindfulness invites us to be fully present. This practice can lead to heightened clarity, improved decision-making, reduced stress, and a deeper appreciation of life's subtleties.

The Principles of Presence, Awareness, and Non-judgment

Three fundamental principles form the bedrock of mindfulness: presence, awareness, and non-judgment.

1. Presence: Being present means devoting our full attention to the current moment. In mindful partnership, this translates to giving our partner our undivided presence when they are speaking, setting aside distractions and the temptation to plan responses in advance. This presence communicates respect and creates a space for genuine connection.

2. Awareness: Mindful awareness involves observing our internal experiences, such as thoughts and emotions, without becoming entangled in them. In relationships, this principle encourages us to recognize our own emotional reactions and patterns, allowing us to respond consciously rather than being carried away by instinctual reactions.

3. Non-judgment: Non-judgmental awareness entails observing experiences without labeling them as good or bad. In the context of mindful partnership, this means approaching our partner's words and actions with an open mind, free from preconceived judgments. This attitude fosters empathy and understanding, enabling us to see things from their perspective.

By integrating these principles into our interactions, we foster an environment of mutual respect and emotional safety. As we cultivate mindfulness within ourselves, we become better equipped to extend this mindful presence to our relationships, enriching our connections and promoting an atmosphere of trust and authenticity.

In the following chapters, we will explore how the principles of mindfulness can be woven into the fabric of relationships, transforming the way we communicate, navigate conflicts, and nurture lasting connections. The journey of mindful partnership begins with these foundational concepts, allowing us to lay the groundwork for more meaningful and harmonious relationships.

3

Cultivating Self-Awareness

In the realm of mindful partnerships, self-awareness serves as a cornerstone for building healthier and more meaningful relationships. By developing a profound understanding of our own thoughts, emotions, and behaviors, we gain the insight necessary to navigate the intricacies of connection and communication. This chapter delves into the significance of self-awareness and presents a range of techniques to foster a deeper understanding of oneself.

The Role of Self-Awareness

Self-awareness is the ability to observe oneself objectively, recognizing thoughts, emotions, and behaviors without judgment. In the context of mindful partnerships, self-awareness plays a pivotal role in several key areas:

1. Emotional Regulation: By understanding our emotional triggers and patterns, we become more adept at managing our reactions. This skill prevents knee-jerk responses during conflicts, fostering a space for thoughtful and empathetic communication.

2. Effective Communication: Self-awareness allows us to communicate our needs, desires, and boundaries with clarity. It enables us to express ourselves authentically while also being attuned to our partner's emotions and responses.

3. Empathy: A deep understanding of our own emotional landscape equips us to empathize with others. When we can identify and relate to our own feelings, we are better positioned to comprehend the feelings of our partners.

4. Personal Growth: Self-awareness is a catalyst for personal growth and development. Recognizing our strengths and areas for improvement fosters an environment where we can continuously evolve, positively impacting our relationships.

Techniques for Developing Self-Awareness

1. Mindful Self-Reflection: Set aside time daily for introspection. Engage in mindfulness practices such as meditation or journaling to explore your thoughts and emotions. This practice cultivates a non-judgmental awareness of your inner world.

2. Emotion Tracking: Keep a journal to record your emotional experiences throughout the day. Note what triggers different emotions and how you respond. Over time, patterns and insights will emerge.

3. Body Awareness: Tune into your body's physical sensations. Often, our bodies provide signals about our emotions before our minds do. Pay attention to tension, relaxation, and other bodily cues.

4. Feedback Seeking: Solicit honest feedback from trusted friends or partners about your behaviors and communication style. This external perspective can shed light on blind spots you might not be aware of.

5. Pause and Reflect: Before reacting to a situation, take a moment to pause. Ask yourself what emotions are arising and why. This brief pause can prevent impulsive reactions driven by unexamined emotions.

6. Mindful Listening: During conversations, practice mindful listening. Focus on the speaker's words without planning your response. This practice not only enhances your understanding but also demonstrates respect to your partner.

7. Self-Compassion: Treat yourself with the same kindness and understanding that you extend to others. Self-compassion creates a nurturing environment for self-awareness to flourish.

By engaging in these techniques, we embark on a journey of self-discovery that extends beyond the individual self. As we deepen our self-awareness, we develop the tools necessary to nurture and sustain mindful partnerships. In the chapters ahead, we will explore how this self-awareness intertwines with empathy, active listening, and effective communication to create the foundation for authentic and enduring connections.

4

Active Listening and Communication

In the intricate dance of relationships, communication serves as the music that guides our steps. Mindful communication, characterized by active listening and a deep sense of presence, has the power to transform interactions from routine exchanges into meaningful exchanges of understanding and empathy. This chapter explores the art of mindful communication and the practice of active listening, unveiling how these skills elevate our connections within mindful partnerships.

The Art of Mindful Communication

Mindful communication is a conscious and intentional approach to exchanging thoughts, feelings, and ideas. It involves being fully present, speaking from a place of authenticity, and listening with genuine attention. This form of communication is grounded in respect and empathy, creating an atmosphere where both partners feel heard and understood.

Active Listening: The Key to Empathy

At the heart of mindful communication lies active listening. Active listening

ACTIVE LISTENING AND COMMUNICATION

goes beyond merely hearing words; it involves being fully engaged and receptive to the speaker's message. This practice necessitates setting aside distractions, suspending judgment, and offering your complete presence. Active listening sends the powerful message that you value the speaker's perspective and are committed to understanding their thoughts and emotions.

The Role of Presence in Understanding and Empathy

Presence is the foundation upon which active listening is built. When we are truly present, we are attuned to the speaker's words, tone, and body language. This heightened awareness enables us to pick up on nuances and unspoken emotions, facilitating a deeper understanding of their experience. Additionally, by being present, we create a safe space for open expression, fostering a sense of trust and emotional intimacy.

Techniques for Mindful Communication and Active Listening

1. Put Away Distractions: During conversations, set aside phones and other distractions to fully engage with the speaker.

2. Maintain Eye Contact: Eye contact communicates attentiveness and respect. It also helps you pick up on nonverbal cues.

3. Practice Reflective Listening: Periodically reflect back what you've heard to ensure understanding. This also lets the speaker know you are actively engaged.

4. Suspend Judgment: Approach conversations without preconceived judgments. This encourages open sharing.

5. Validate Emotions: Acknowledge the speaker's emotions, even if you don't agree with their viewpoint. This validation fosters a sense of empathy.

6. Empathetic Responses: Respond with empathy by acknowledging the speaker's emotions and demonstrating that you understand their perspective.

7. Mindful Breathing: Before responding, take a mindful breath to collect your thoughts and respond thoughtfully rather than reactively.

Creating Meaningful Connections

Mindful communication and active listening work in tandem to build bridges of understanding and empathy within relationships. By fostering an environment where each partner feels valued and heard, mindful partnerships flourish. The practice of presence and active listening not only enhances your connection but also sets the stage for collaborative problem-solving, conflict resolution, and a deeper emotional bond.

In the forthcoming chapters, we will explore how these principles integrate into conflict resolution, negotiation, and shared decision-making, providing you with the tools to navigate challenges and cultivate lasting harmony within your relationships.

5

Emotional Intelligence and Empathy

In the intricate tapestry of relationships, emotional intelligence and empathy are the threads that weave the fabric of understanding and connection. These qualities form the bedrock of mindful partnerships, enabling individuals to navigate the emotional landscapes of both themselves and their partners with grace and authenticity. This chapter delves into the development of emotional intelligence as a cornerstone of mindful partnership, while also exploring how fostering empathy connects partners on a deeper emotional level.

Developing Emotional Intelligence

Emotional intelligence, often referred to as EQ, is the ability to recognize, understand, manage, and effectively use one's own emotions, as well as to perceive and influence the emotions of others. Within mindful partnerships, EQ serves as a guiding light, offering the following benefits:

1. Self-Awareness: Emotional intelligence empowers individuals to identify and comprehend their emotions and triggers. This heightened self-awareness forms the foundation for authentic communication and emotional regulation.

2. Empathy: A key component of EQ, empathy enables partners to place themselves in each other's shoes, fostering a sense of understanding and compassion. It bridges the gap between experiences and cultivates a deep emotional connection.

3. Effective Communication: Emotional intelligence enhances the ability to communicate feelings and needs clearly and respectfully. This skill prevents misunderstandings and encourages open dialogue.

4. Conflict Resolution: EQ equips individuals to approach conflicts with emotional maturity. By managing their own emotions and perceiving their partner's feelings, they can navigate disagreements with empathy and a focus on resolution.

Fostering Empathy

Empathy is the cornerstone of genuine human connection. It involves not only understanding someone's emotions but also feeling them to some degree. In mindful partnerships, empathy creates a profound emotional bond by:

1. Listening Actively: Actively listening to your partner's words, tone, and nonverbal cues allows you to discern their emotions and experiences.

2. Seeking to Understand: Make an effort to understand your partner's perspective, even if you don't agree with it. This validates their emotions and shows that you value their feelings.

3. Expressing Understanding: Verbalize your understanding of your partner's emotions. This acknowledgment demonstrates your empathy and fosters a sense of validation.

4. Sharing Emotions: Openly share your own emotions with your partner. This vulnerability paves the way for mutual emotional sharing and a deeper

connection.

Techniques for Developing Emotional Intelligence and Empathy

1. Self-Reflection: Regularly reflect on your own emotional experiences and reactions. This practice enhances self-awareness and empathy for yourself and others.

2. Mindful Observation: Observe your partner's facial expressions, body language, and tone during conversations. These cues offer insight into their emotions.

3. Ask Open-Ended Questions: Encourage your partner to share their feelings by asking open-ended questions that go beyond surface-level responses.

4. Practice Perspective-Taking: Imagine how a situation might feel from your partner's point of view. This exercise enhances empathy by stepping into their emotional shoes.

5. Reflect on Shared Experiences: Recall moments when you've felt similar emotions to your partner's. This can foster a deeper understanding of their feelings.

By developing emotional intelligence and fostering empathy, you lay the groundwork for a richer, more authentic connection within your mindful partnership. The fusion of emotional awareness and genuine understanding serves as the catalyst for transformative interactions, nurturing a bond that can withstand the tests of time and challenges. As we venture forward, we'll explore how these qualities illuminate the path to conflict resolution, negotiation, and shared decision-making in the context of mindful partnerships.

6

Navigating Conflict Mindfully

Conflict, though inevitable in any relationship, is also a crossroads where growth and understanding can flourish. By approaching conflicts with mindfulness, we transform what could be destructive clashes into opportunities for deeper connection and resolution. This chapter explores approaches to addressing conflicts and disagreements mindfully, along with strategies for maintaining composure and resolving issues constructively within the context of mindful partnerships.

Approaches to Addressing Conflicts with Mindfulness

1. Pause and Breathe: When conflict arises, take a mindful pause before reacting. Breathe deeply and give yourself a moment to collect your thoughts and emotions.

2. Choose Words Mindfully: Speak consciously and respectfully. Avoid blame or defensiveness, focusing on "I" statements to express your feelings and needs.

3. Listen Actively: Give your partner your full attention when they express

their perspective. Put aside your own thoughts and truly listen to their words and emotions.

4. Empathize: Cultivate empathy by understanding your partner's feelings and perspective. Reflect on how they might be experiencing the situation.

Strategies for Constructive Conflict Resolution

1. Find Common Ground: Identify shared values or goals that both you and your partner can agree on. This common ground can serve as a foundation for resolving the conflict.

2. Seek Understanding: Ask open-ended questions to gain insight into your partner's viewpoint. Understand the underlying emotions and concerns driving their perspective.

3. Stay Present: During the conflict, remain present and focused on the issue at hand. Avoid bringing up past conflicts or unrelated matters.

4. Use "I" Statements: Communicate your feelings using "I" statements, which convey your emotions without assigning blame. For example, say "I feel hurt when…" instead of "You always do…"

5. Practice Active Problem-Solving: Collaboratively brainstorm solutions to the conflict. Approach the situation as a team, aiming for a win-win outcome.

6. Take Breaks: If the conflict becomes heated, it's okay to take a break. Step away to regain composure and return to the conversation when emotions have cooled.

7. Acknowledge Emotions: Validate each other's emotions, even if you don't agree with each other. Acknowledging feelings creates a sense of understanding and safety.

Maintaining Composure in Heated Moments

1. Mindful Breathing: When emotions escalate, focus on your breath. Deep, mindful breaths can help calm your nervous system and restore clarity.

2. Grounding Techniques: Engage your senses to stay present. Focus on the sensation of your feet on the ground or the feeling of an object in your hand.

3. Self-Compassion: Be kind to yourself and your partner during conflicts. Recognize that emotions can be intense but also transient.

4. Use Humor: Lightening the mood with gentle humor can diffuse tension and create space for a more constructive conversation.

5. Practice Acceptance: Not all conflicts will result in complete agreement. Sometimes, the goal is to find a compromise that both partners can accept.

Approaching conflicts mindfully within a partnership transforms them from battles into opportunities for growth and connection. By implementing these strategies and techniques, you empower yourself and your partner to navigate challenges in a way that preserves the bond you've worked so hard to build. As we move forward, we'll delve into negotiation and shared decision-making within mindful partnerships, building upon the foundation of mindful communication and conflict resolution.

7

Mindful Intimacy

Intimacy, whether physical or emotional, forms the heart of a mindful partnership. The practice of mindfulness extends its gentle touch into the realm of intimacy, deepening connections and fostering vulnerability through present-moment awareness. This chapter explores how to bring mindfulness to both physical and emotional intimacy, enriching the fabric of your relationship and cultivating a profound sense of connection.

Mindfulness in Physical Intimacy

1. Presence: Approach physical intimacy with a heightened sense of presence. Allow yourself to fully experience the sensations, emotions, and connection that the moment holds.

2. Sensory Awareness: Engage your senses during intimate moments. Pay attention to touch, taste, smell, sight, and sound, amplifying the richness of the experience.

3. Non-Judgment: Release self-criticism and judgment. Embrace your body and your partner's body without comparing them to external standards.

4. Communication: Maintain open communication with your partner about your desires, boundaries, and preferences. Mindful communication paves the way for greater intimacy.

5. Connection: Use eye contact, gentle touch, and affectionate gestures to deepen your emotional and physical connection during intimate moments.

Mindfulness in Emotional Intimacy

1. Vulnerability: Practice vulnerability by sharing your true thoughts and emotions with your partner. Approach emotional intimacy with an open heart.

2. Active Listening: When your partner shares their emotions, listen with undivided attention. Offer empathy and understanding without immediately jumping to solutions.

3. Validation: Validate your partner's feelings and experiences. Let them know that their emotions are heard and respected.

4. Empathy: Put yourself in your partner's shoes to understand their emotional world. This deepens your emotional connection and fosters empathy.

5. Reflective Sharing: Share your own emotions and experiences with authenticity. Vulnerability encourages reciprocal sharing and strengthens the emotional bond.

The Power of Present-Moment Awareness

Present-moment awareness infuses both physical and emotional intimacy with a transformative quality. By being fully present with your partner, you create a space free from distractions, worries, and judgments. This allows intimacy to blossom in its purest form, deepening the sense of connection and authenticity between you.

Cultivating Mindful Intimacy

1. Set the Scene: Create an environment conducive to mindfulness and intimacy. This might include soft lighting, comfortable surroundings, and calming scents.

2. Breath Awareness: Use your breath as an anchor for staying present. Focus on your breath to quiet the mind and enhance the depth of your connection.

3. Practice Mindful Touch: During physical intimacy, focus on each touch and sensation. Let go of distractions and immerse yourself in the experience.

4. Embrace Imperfections: Both physical bodies and emotional landscapes are imperfect. Embrace and celebrate these imperfections, as they are part of the beautiful tapestry of your partnership.

5. Express Gratitude: After intimate moments, express gratitude for the connection and the shared experience. Gratitude enhances the emotional bond between partners.

Bringing mindfulness into your physical and emotional intimacy transforms these moments from routine occurrences into sacred connections. By nurturing this mindful intimacy, you nurture the heart of your mindful partnership, fostering a bond that is characterized by authenticity, vulnerability, and a deep sense of being seen and valued. As we journey further, we'll explore shared decision-making, the integration of mindfulness into daily life, and the ways in which a mindful partnership continues to evolve and thrive.

8

Letting Go of Expectations

Expectations, though often well-intentioned, can cast a shadow over relationships, obscuring the beauty of the present moment. The practice of letting go of expectations is a fundamental aspect of cultivating a mindful partnership. In this chapter, we'll explore the impact of expectations on relationships, the steps to release them, and the profound benefits of embracing acceptance and appreciating each moment as it unfolds.

The Impact of Expectations on Relationships

Expectations can lead to a variety of challenges within relationships:

1. Unmet Expectations: When expectations are not met, disappointment and resentment can arise, eroding the foundation of the partnership.

2. Loss of Authenticity: Expectations may pressure partners to conform to specific roles or behaviors, suppressing their authentic selves.

3. Missed Opportunities: Focusing on future outcomes can lead to missing out on the richness of the present moment.

4. Communication Barriers: Unspoken or mismatched expectations can lead to misunderstandings and miscommunication.

Releasing Expectations

1. Self-Reflection: Examine your own expectations and where they originate. Consider whether they are realistic and necessary.

2. Open Dialogue: Engage in open conversations with your partner about expectations. Align your mutual expectations to foster clarity and understanding.

3. Shift Focus: Shift your focus from future outcomes to the present moment. Embrace the experience as it unfolds rather than fixating on desired results.

4. Practice Flexibility: Embrace flexibility in your expectations. Allow for spontaneity and organic growth within the relationship.

5. Cultivate Gratitude: Shift your attention towards appreciating what the relationship offers in the present moment, rather than focusing on what's lacking.

Embracing Acceptance and Appreciation

1. Acceptance: Accept the imperfections and complexities of your partner and the relationship. Embrace the truth that both of you are constantly evolving.

2. Gratitude Practice: Cultivate a gratitude practice that focuses on the positive aspects of your partner and the partnership. This practice nurtures a sense of contentment.

3. Mindful Presence: Be fully present with your partner, without judgment or attachment to outcomes. Engage in shared moments with undivided

attention.

4. Letting Go of Comparison: Release the habit of comparing your relationship to others. Your journey is unique and should be appreciated for its individuality.

Benefits of Letting Go

1. Greater Freedom: Letting go of expectations frees you to experience the relationship as it is, allowing for spontaneity and authenticity.

2. Reduced Conflict: Releasing rigid expectations reduces potential sources of conflict and fosters a more harmonious environment.

3. Deeper Connection: Embracing each moment as it is deepens your emotional connection, fostering authenticity and vulnerability.

4. Enhanced Well-Being: Letting go of expectations reduces stress and anxiety, contributing to your overall well-being.

By embracing acceptance, releasing expectations, and appreciating the beauty of each moment, you nurture a mindful partnership that thrives on authenticity and connection. Letting go allows your relationship to flourish organically, unburdened by the weight of unrealized expectations. As we journey onward, we'll explore the integration of mindfulness into various aspects of life and relationships, helping you build a strong foundation for a fulfilling and lasting partnership.

9

Balancing Individuality and Togetherness

The dance between individuality and togetherness is a delicate yet essential aspect of mindful partnerships. Striking the right balance between personal growth and nurturing the relationship is a dynamic journey that requires conscious awareness and intentional effort. In this chapter, we'll explore how to find equilibrium between these two elements, fostering personal development while also enriching the partnership.

Nurturing Personal Growth

1. Self-Care: Prioritize self-care routines that nurture your physical, emotional, and mental well-being. A balanced individual contributes positively to the relationship.

2. Personal Goals: Set and pursue personal goals that align with your passions and aspirations. Share these goals with your partner to foster mutual understanding.

3. Alone Time: Create space for solitude and introspection. This allows you

to recharge and develop a deeper sense of self-awareness.

4. Hobbies and Interests: Engage in activities and hobbies that bring you joy and fulfillment, even if they are pursued independently.

Supporting Each Other's Aspirations

1. Active Listening: Be genuinely interested in your partner's dreams and aspirations. Listen actively and offer encouragement.

2. Empathetic Support: Show empathy towards your partner's challenges and setbacks. Offer a supportive presence during moments of difficulty.

3. Collaborative Planning: Explore opportunities for mutual growth. Plan shared experiences that align with both of your aspirations.

4. Respect for Differences: Understand that you and your partner may have different paths and passions. Respect these differences and celebrate each other's uniqueness.

Finding the Equilibrium

1. Open Communication: Regularly discuss your individual aspirations and how they align with the partnership. Address any concerns or challenges that arise.

2. Scheduled Check-Ins: Set aside time for check-ins to discuss your personal goals and how they're impacting the relationship. This fosters understanding and connection.

3. Flexibility: Adapt to the evolving needs of both yourself and the partnership. Sometimes, adjustments are necessary to maintain balance.

4. Shared Values: Identify shared values that serve as the foundation of your partnership. These values can guide decisions that impact personal growth and the relationship.

Benefits of Balance

1. Enhanced Connection: Balancing individuality and togetherness strengthens your emotional connection, as you both have the space to grow and evolve.

2. Resilience: When both partners are fulfilled as individuals, the partnership becomes more resilient in the face of challenges.

3. Mutual Support: Supporting each other's aspirations fosters a sense of mutual respect and admiration, strengthening the partnership.

4. Harmonious Growth: Achieving equilibrium ensures that personal growth and relationship nurturing occur in tandem, promoting harmony.

By intentionally navigating the delicate dance of individuality and togetherness, you create a mindful partnership that flourishes through mutual growth and shared experiences. Balancing personal aspirations with the collective journey cultivates a relationship that thrives on understanding, support, and the celebration of each partner's unique path. As we continue forward, we'll explore the practical integration of mindfulness into everyday life, solidifying the foundations of your mindful partnership.

10

Mindful Decision-Making

In the intricate tapestry of a mindful partnership, decision-making forms the threads that weave shared experiences and shape the trajectory of the relationship. The art of mindful decision-making empowers couples to navigate choices with clarity, aligning actions with shared values and aspirations. In this chapter, we'll explore the significance of conscious decision-making, how to make choices that resonate with the partnership, and the role of mindfulness in avoiding impulsive decisions.

The Significance of Mindful Decision-Making

1. Alignment with Values: Mindful decision-making ensures that choices are aligned with the shared values and principles that underpin the partnership.

2. Shared Goals: Conscious choices are driven by the vision of a collective future, fostering a sense of togetherness and purpose.

3. Preventing Conflicts: By considering the impact of decisions on both partners, conflicts arising from divergent paths can be minimized.

4. Strengthening Trust: Mindful decision-making nurtures trust, as partners feel that their perspectives and needs are considered in every choice.

Making Choices Aligned with the Partnership

1. Open Dialogue: Engage in open conversations about important decisions. Ensure both partners have a voice and are heard.

2. Shared Vision: Regularly revisit and discuss your shared vision for the partnership. This vision serves as a compass for decision-making.

3. Consider Impact: Reflect on how a decision will impact both yourself and your partner. Consider short-term and long-term implications.

4. Collaborative Problem-Solving: Approach decisions as a team. Collaboratively brainstorm solutions that align with your shared goals.

The Role of Mindfulness in Decision-Making

1. Pause and Reflect: Before making decisions, pause to center yourself. Reflect on your motivations, values, and how the choice aligns with your vision.

2. Notice Impulses: Mindfulness helps you become aware of impulsive reactions. Observe your thoughts and emotions without immediately acting on them.

3. Clarity of Thought: Mindfulness clears mental clutter, allowing you to make decisions from a place of clarity rather than reactivity.

4. Staying Present: Being present during the decision-making process prevents you from getting lost in worries about the future or regrets from the past.

Strategies for Mindful Decision-Making

1. Mindful Breathing: Before making a decision, take a few mindful breaths to ground yourself and bring your focus to the present moment.

2. Check-In with Emotions: Notice your emotional state. If you're feeling anxious or rushed, consider postponing the decision until you're in a calmer state of mind.

3. Create Space: Allow yourself time to make decisions. Avoid rushing or making choices under pressure.

4. Consider Alternatives: Explore different options before settling on a decision. This prevents impulsiveness and encourages thoughtful consideration.

Benefits of Mindful Decision-Making

1. Harmonious Choices: Mindful decision-making fosters choices that resonate with the partnership, leading to a harmonious and fulfilling journey.

2. Mutual Empowerment: Both partners feel empowered and valued when decisions are made with consideration for each other's needs.

3. Enhanced Communication: The process of discussing decisions mindfully promotes open communication and understanding.

4. Stronger Bonds: Making choices that honor the partnership strengthens the emotional bond and trust between partners.

By infusing mindfulness into the decision-making process, you ensure that your choices contribute to the growth and success of your mindful partnership. As you continue to navigate life's decisions together, remember that each choice is an opportunity to nurture the unique connection you've cultivated.

In our final chapters, we'll explore ways to integrate mindfulness seamlessly into daily life, allowing your partnership to flourish with authenticity and intentionality.

11

Creating Mindful Rituals

In the canvas of a mindful partnership, daily routines and rituals serve as brushstrokes that paint a picture of shared experiences and deep connection. By infusing mindfulness into these rituals, couples can cultivate a sense of presence and intentionality, enhancing their bond and fostering a shared sense of mindfulness. This chapter delves into the art of creating mindful rituals as a couple, exploring ways to weave mindfulness into your daily lives.

The Power of Mindful Rituals

1. Connection: Mindful rituals provide dedicated time for partners to connect, even in the midst of busy schedules.

2. Intimacy: These rituals encourage vulnerability and intimacy, as partners share moments of authenticity and presence.

3. Stress Relief: Mindful rituals offer an oasis of calm, helping both partners reduce stress and restore a sense of balance.

4. Shared Presence: Engaging in mindful rituals fosters a shared sense of presence, deepening your connection on a profound level.

Infusing Mindfulness into Daily Routines

1. Morning Reflection: Start your day with a moment of reflection and gratitude. Share something you're grateful for with your partner.

2. Mindful Meals: During meals, practice mindful eating by savoring each bite and engaging in unhurried conversation.

3. Technology-Free Time: Designate technology-free periods where you can fully engage with each other without distractions.

4. Evening Wind-Down: Before bed, engage in a relaxing activity together, such as meditation, gentle stretching, or a calming walk.

Creating Mindful Rituals Together

1. Intention Setting: Begin each ritual with a shared intention. This aligns both partners and sets the tone for the experience.

2. Breath Synchronization: Practice synchronized breathing to cultivate a sense of unity and connection.

3. Nature Walks: Take mindful walks in nature, engaging your senses and appreciating the beauty around you.

4. Mindful Listening: Dedicate time for mindful listening. One partner speaks while the other listens attentively, without interrupting or offering advice.

Nurturing Connection Through Mindful Rituals

MINDFUL PARTNERSHIP: PRACTICING PRESENCE IN RELATIONSHIPS

1. Shared Gratitude: Express gratitude for each other within your rituals. This reaffirms your appreciation and love.

2. Playful Moments: Infuse playfulness into your rituals, fostering a light-hearted and joyful atmosphere.

3. Emotional Check-Ins: Regularly check in with each other about your emotions and experiences. This deepens your emotional connection.

4. Shared Goals: Use your mindful rituals as a space to discuss and reaffirm your shared goals and vision for the partnership.

The Transformative Impact

1. Deeper Connection: Engaging in mindful rituals allows you to connect on a more profound level, creating lasting memories.

2. Enhanced Communication: These rituals foster open communication and encourage vulnerability.

3. Stress Reduction: Mindful rituals offer moments of respite from the demands of daily life, promoting relaxation and stress reduction.

4. Nurtured Bond: The intentional nature of these rituals nurtures the bond between partners, contributing to a strong and enduring partnership.

By intentionally weaving mindfulness into your daily routines and creating meaningful rituals, you invite a sense of presence, connection, and authenticity into your partnership. These moments of shared mindfulness can be a guiding light that illuminates your journey together, enhancing the fabric of your relationship with each brushstroke of intentionality. As we conclude our exploration, remember that the path of a mindful partnership is an ongoing journey, enriched by your commitment to mindfulness, authenticity, and shared growth.

12

Sustaining a Mindful Partnership

As you stand at the crossroads of your mindful partnership journey, it's essential to reflect on the path you've traversed and look ahead to the road that stretches into the future. Sustaining a mindful partnership is an ongoing commitment that requires continuous effort and dedication. In this final chapter, we'll reflect on the journey you've undertaken, offer guidance for maintaining a lifelong commitment to mindfulness in your partnership, and remind you of the enduring beauty that mindful connections can bring.

Reflecting on the Journey

1. Celebrating Progress: Take a moment to celebrate how far you've come. Reflect on the growth you've experienced individually and as a couple.

2. Learning from Challenges: Consider the challenges you've faced and the lessons you've learned. Challenges are opportunities for growth and deeper understanding.

3. Cherishing Memories: Recall the meaningful moments you've shared

on this journey. These memories are the building blocks of your mindful partnership.

4. Appreciating Connection: Reflect on the emotional intimacy and connection you've cultivated. This is the heart of your mindful partnership.

Maintaining a Lifelong Commitment

1. Continued Communication: Keep the lines of communication open. Regularly check in with each other about your thoughts, feelings, and aspirations.

2. Shared Mindfulness: Continue to infuse mindfulness into your daily lives. Engage in mindful activities and conversations that nurture your connection.

3. Adapting Together: As life evolves, be willing to adapt your mindfulness practices to align with your changing circumstances and goals.

4. Prioritizing Self-Care: Individual self-care remains important. Nurture your well-being to ensure you bring your best self to the partnership.

Embracing the Beauty of Mindful Connection

1. Authenticity: The beauty of mindful partnership lies in its authenticity. Continue to be your true selves, supporting each other's growth.

2. Gentle Presence: Offer each other the gift of presence, especially during challenging times. Your support can be a source of comfort and strength.

3. Shared Vision: Revisit your shared vision and goals regularly. This vision guides your journey and keeps you aligned.

4. Gratitude: Cultivate an ongoing sense of gratitude for the relationship

you've built. Gratitude fuels positivity and appreciation.

The Endless Journey

As you move forward on your journey of sustaining a mindful partnership, remember that mindfulness is not a destination but an ever-evolving way of being. Each day presents an opportunity to deepen your connection, learn from each other, and continue growing individually and together. The beauty of a mindful partnership is that it becomes a source of strength and inspiration, a place where you both can find solace, joy, and a profound sense of belonging.

Embrace the journey with an open heart, and let the principles of mindfulness guide you. Your commitment to authenticity, presence, and growth will weave a tapestry of connection that only becomes richer with time. As you move forward, know that the path you've chosen is one of immense beauty and transformative power—a path that leads to a lifetime of love, understanding, and shared mindfulness.

Conclusion: Embracing Mindful Connections in Relationships

In the intricate dance of relationships, the art of practicing presence is a transformative force that elevates connections from mere interactions to profound bonds of understanding, empathy, and growth. Throughout this journey, we've explored the key principles of cultivating mindfulness in relationships, each step revealing the power of being fully present, authentic, and intentional. As we conclude this exploration, let's revisit these principles and encourage you to embrace mindfulness in your partnerships for a more fulfilling and lasting connection.

The Key Principles of Mindful Connections

1. Presence: Being fully present with your partner, both in moments of joy

and during challenges, creates a foundation of authentic connection.

2. Authenticity: Embracing vulnerability and authenticity fosters deeper understanding and a sense of safety within the partnership.

3. Active Listening: The art of active listening, with empathy and non-judgment, cultivates a space where partners feel heard and valued.

4. Emotional Intelligence: Developing emotional intelligence nurtures understanding and compassion, allowing for healthier conflict resolution.

5. Empathy: Empathy bridges the gap between experiences, enhancing the emotional connection and fostering a profound bond.

6. Balancing Individuality and Togetherness: Finding equilibrium between personal growth and partnership supports both individual aspirations and the relationship's evolution.

7. Mindful Decision-Making: Infusing mindfulness into decision-making aligns actions with shared values and goals, promoting harmony and understanding.

8. Mindful Rituals: Creating mindful rituals allows partners to connect and engage in shared experiences that deepen the bond of the relationship.

Embrace Mindfulness for a Fulfilling Connection

As you move forward on your journey, remember that practicing mindfulness is not about perfection but about intentionality. Integrate these principles into your relationship with the understanding that mindfulness is an ongoing practice—a way of being that requires conscious effort and dedication. By doing so, you create a partnership that is characterized by depth, authenticity, and mutual growth.

Let each interaction become an opportunity to embody presence and empathy. When challenges arise, approach them with open hearts and the intention to understand before seeking to be understood. Let your shared mindfulness be a guiding light, illuminating your path even in moments of uncertainty.

As you embrace the art of mindful connections, you'll find that the threads of understanding, empathy, and love weave a tapestry that's as intricate as it is beautiful. Your commitment to practicing presence will continue to enrich your relationship, creating a bond that stands strong even in the face of life's trials. With each mindful step you take, you create a legacy of love, authenticity, and lasting connection that will resonate through time.

www.ingramcontent.com/pod-product-compliance
Lightning Source LLC
LaVergne TN
LVHW010438070526
838199LV00066B/6074